SOMETHING FOR BOYS

Arranged by DAN COATES
for easy piano

Project Manager: CAROL CUELLAR
Art Design: CARMEN FORTUNATO

© 1999 WARNER BROS. PUBLICATIONS
All Rights Reserved

Dan Coates

One of today's foremost personalities in the field of printed music, Dan Coates has been providing teachers and professional musicians with quality piano material since 1975. Equally adept in arranging for beginners or accomplished musicians, his Big Note, Easy Piano and Professional Touch arrangements have made a significant contribution to the industry.

Born in Syracuse, New York, Dan began to play piano at the age of four. By the time he was 15, he'd won a New York State competition for music composers. After high school graduation, he toured the United States, Canada and Europe as an arranger and pianist with the world-famous group Up With People.

Dan settled in Miami, Florida, where he studied piano with Ivan Davis at the University of Miami while playing professionally throughout southern Florida. To date, his performance credits include appearances on "Murphy Brown" and "My Sister Sam" and at the Opening Ceremonies of the 1984 Summer Olympics in Los Angeles. Dan has also accompanied such artists as Dusty Springfield and Charlotte Rae.

In 1982, Dan began his association with Warner Bros. Publications—an association that has produced more than four hundred Dan Coates books and sheets. Throughout the year, he conducts piano workshops nationwide, during which he demonstrates his popular arrangements.

CONTENTS

From the Lucasfilm Ltd. Production "STAR WARS" - A Twentieth Century-Fox Release.

CANTINA BAND

Music by
JOHN WILLIAMS
Arranged by DAN COATES

Brightly ($\quad$ = 100)

(L.H. staccato throughout)

6

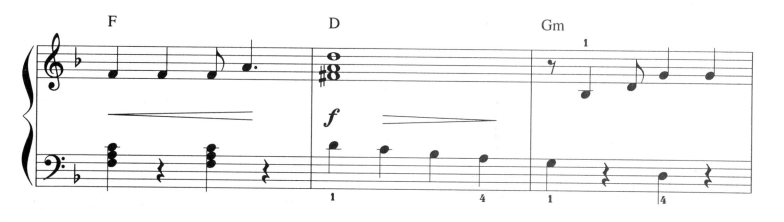

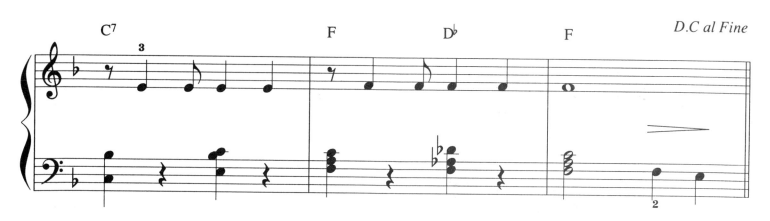

From the Motion Picture "BATMAN"™

THE BATMAN THEME

Music Composed by
DANNY ELFMAN
Arranged by DAN COATES

The Batman Theme - 5 - 1

The Batman Theme - 5 - 2

From the Lucasfilm Ltd. Production ''RETURN OF THE JEDI'' - A Twentieth Century-Fox Release.

EWOK CELEBRATION

Ewokese Lyrics by BEN BURTT
Original English Lyrics by JOSEPH WILLIAMS

Music by
JOHN WILLIAMS
Arranged by DAN COATES

Ewok Celebration - 5 - 1

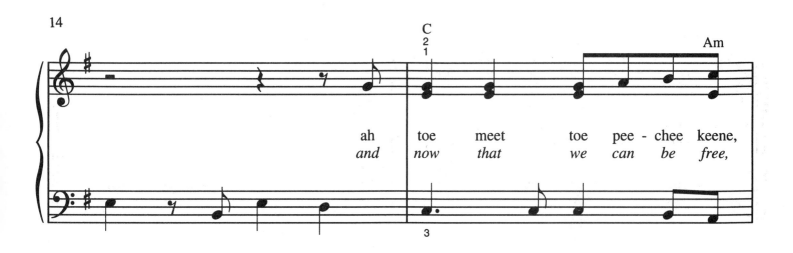

ah   toe   meet   toe   pee - chee   keene,
and   now   that   we   can   be   free,

g' - noop   dock   fling   oh_____   ah._____
it's   time   to   cel - e - brate._____

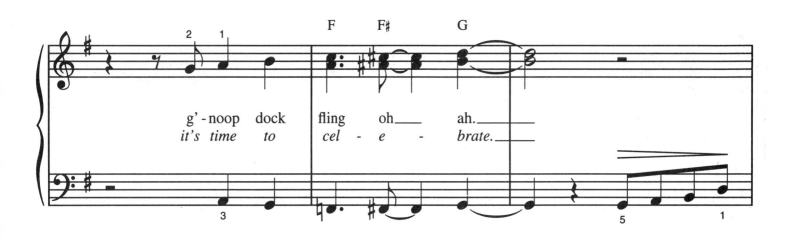

Coat - ee chah   tu   yub_____   nub;   coat - ee chah   tu   yah -
Cel - e - brate   the   free - dom;   cel - e - brate   the   pow -

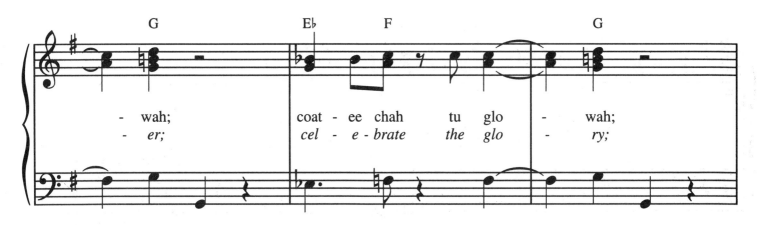

- wah;   coat - ee chah   tu   glo - wah;
- er;   cel - e - brate   the   glo - ry;

al - lay loo___ ta nuv.
cel - e - brate___ the love.
cresc.

Glo - wah,
Pow - er,
eee chop glo - wah;
we got pow - er;

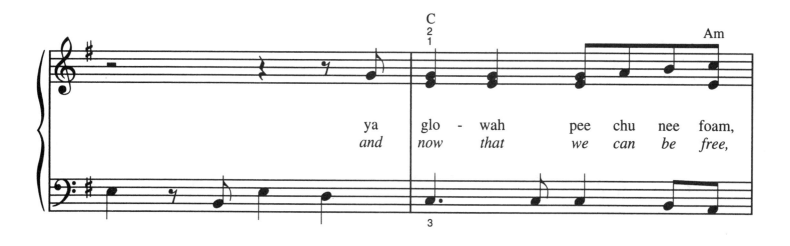

ya glo - wah pee chu nee foam,
and now that we can be free,

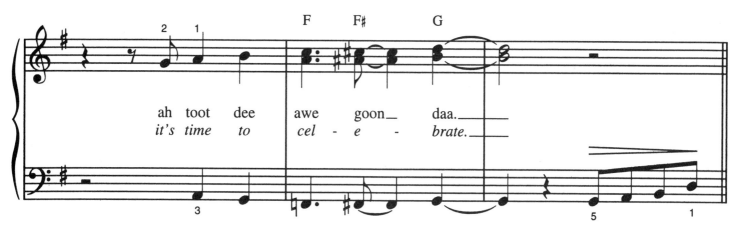

ah toot dee awe goon___ daa.___
it's time to cel - e - brate.

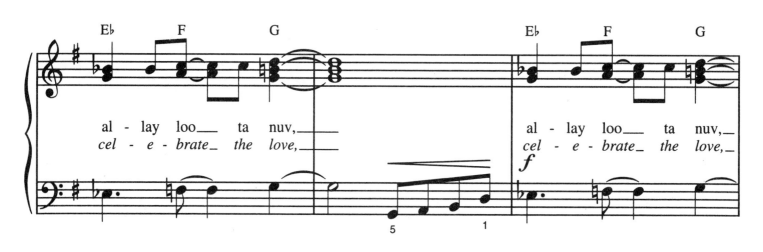

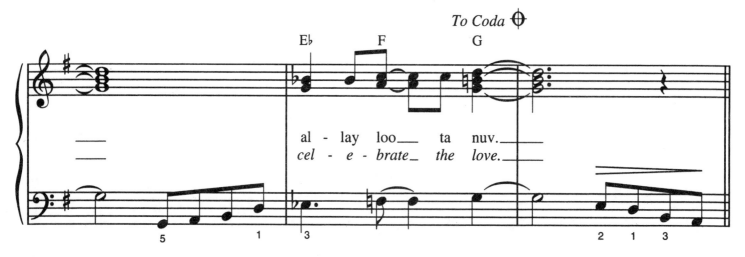

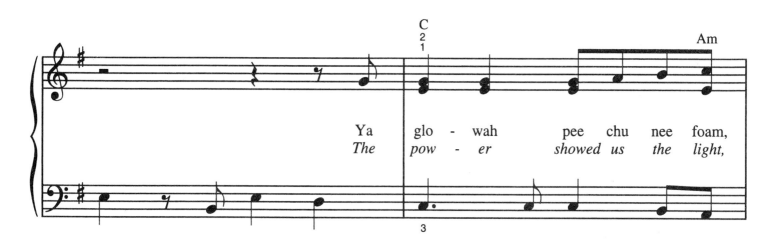

GOTHAM CITY

Words and Music by
R. KELLY
Arranged by DAN COATES

Looking over the skyline of the city,
Sleeping awake because of fear,
now quiet nights in the midst of crime.
children are drowning in their tears.
Next door to happiness lives sorrow, and
We need a place where we can go, a land where

20

I BELIEVE I CAN FLY

Words and Music by
R. KELLY
Arranged by DAN COATES

From Touchstone Pictures' "ARMAGEDDON"

I DON'T WANT TO MISS A THING

Words and Music by
DIANE WARREN
Arranged by DAN COATES

I'LL BE THERE FOR YOU
Theme From "FRIENDS"

Words by
DAVID CRANE, MARTA KAUFFMAN, ALLEE WILLIS,
PHIL SOLEM and DANNY WILDE

Music by
MICHAEL SKLOFF
Arranged by DAN COATES

I'll Be There for You - 6 - 1

I'll Be There for You - 6 - 2

From the Lucasfilm Ltd. Production "THE EMPIRE STRIKES BACK" - A Twentieth Century-Fox Release.

THE IMPERIAL MARCH
(Darth Vader's Theme)

Music by
JOHN WILLIAMS
Arranged by DAN COATES

Steady march tempo

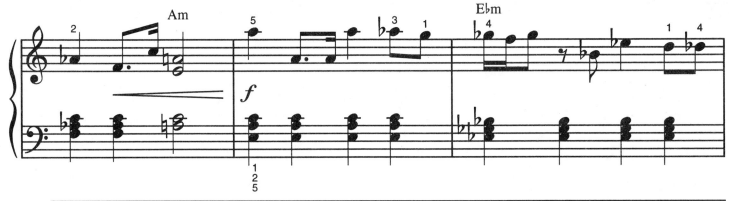

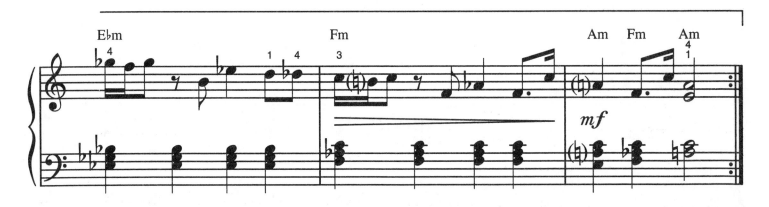

The Imperial March - 2 - 1

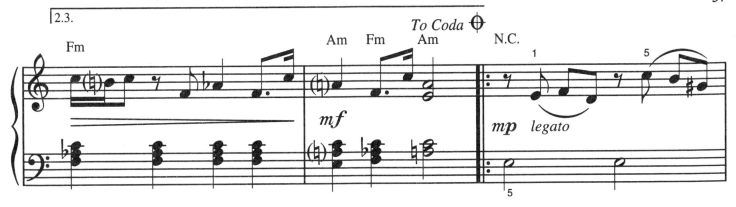

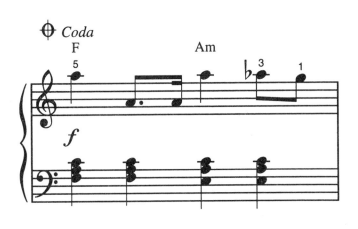

The Imperial March - 2 - 2

From the TV Show "PEANUTS SPECIAL"

LINUS AND LUCY

By VINCE GUARALDI
Arranged by DAN COATES

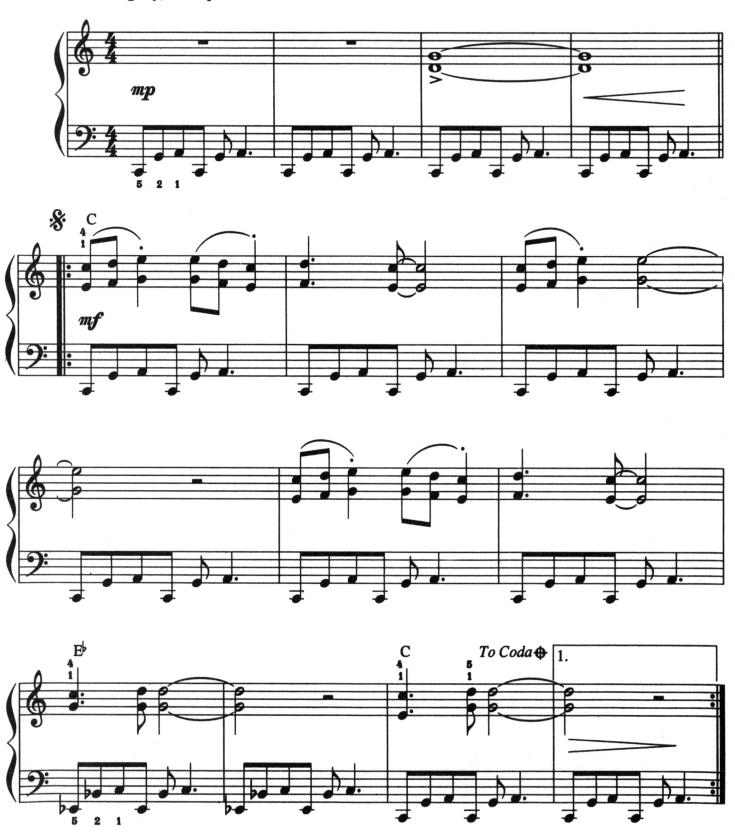

Linus and Lucy - 2 - 1

Linus and Lucy - 2 - 2

***From the Lucasfilm Ltd. Productions "STAR WARS", "THE EMPIRE SRIKES BACK"
and "RETURN OF THE JEDI" - Twentieth Century-Fox Releases.***

STAR WARS
(Main Theme)

Music by
JOHN WILLLIAMS
Arranged by DAN COATES

Star Wars - 2 -1

CANON IN D

JOHANN PACHELBEL
(1653-1706)
Arranged by DAN COATES

Canon in D - 4 - 1

Canon in D - 4 - 2

44

Canon in D - 4 - 4

From the Original Motion Picture Soundtrack "8 SECONDS"

LANE'S THEME

Composed by
BILL CONTI
Arranged by DAN COATES

Lane's Theme - 3 - 1

RAGTIME

Lyrics by
LYNN AHRENS

Music by
STEPHEN FLAHERTY
Arranged by DAN COATES

Ragtime - 5 - 1

And there was dis - tant mu - sic, skip - ping a beat, ___ sing - ing

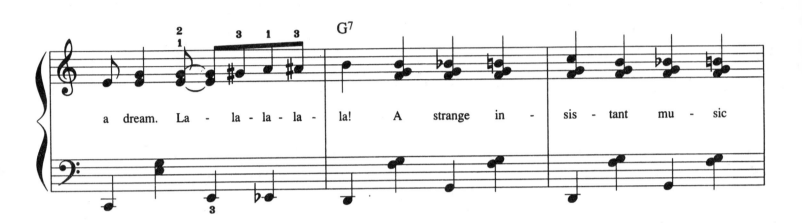

a dream. La - la - la - la - la! A strange in - sis - tant mu - sic

put - ting out heat, ___ pick - ing up steam. La - la - la - la - la! The sound of

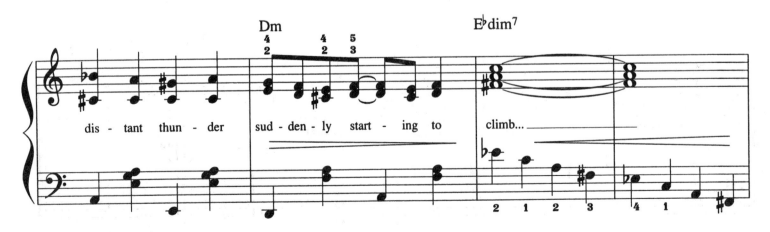

dis - tant thun - der sud - den - ly start - ing to climb... ___

Theme Song from the Mirisch-G&E Production "THE PINK PANTHER," a United Artists Release

THE PINK PANTHER

Music by
HENRY MANCINI
Arranged by DAN COATES

Mysterioso ♩ = 110

The Pink Panther - 2 - 1

The Pink Panther - 2 - 2

MORE THAN WORDS

Lyrics and Music by
BETTENCOURT, CHERONE
Arranged by DAN COATES

Moderate rock ballad ♩ = 92

58

Verse 2:
Now that I have tried to talk to you
And make you understand,
All you have to do is close your eyes
And just reach out your hands
And touch me, hold me close, don't ever let me go.
More than words is all I ever needed you to show.
Then you wouldn't have to say
That you love me, 'cause I'd already know.

From the Warner Bros. Motion Picture "SUPERMAN"

THEME FROM "SUPERMAN"

Music by
JOHN WILLIAMS
Arranged by DAN COATES

Theme From "Superman" - 3 - 1

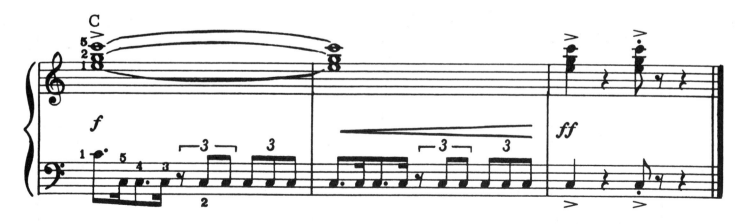

Theme From "Superman" - 3 - 3

TAKE ME OUT TO THE BALL GAME

Words by JACK NORWORTH
Music by ALBERT VON TILZER
Arranged by DAN COATES

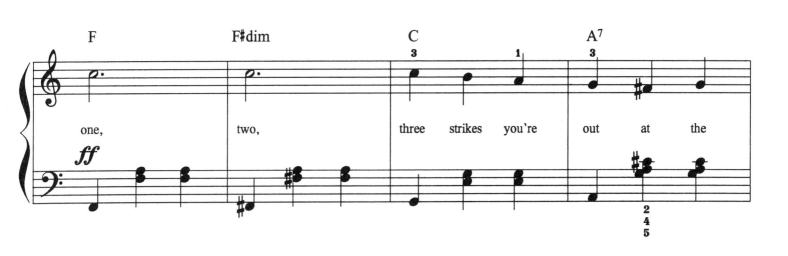

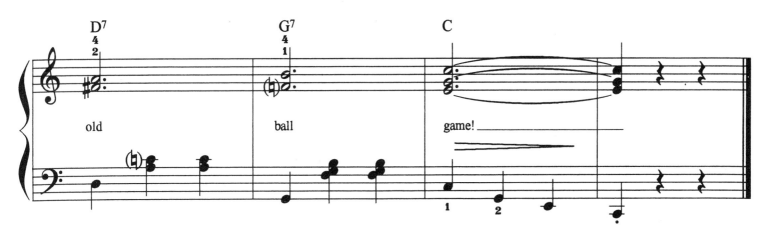

From the Twentieth Century-Fox Motion Picture

THAT THING YOU DO!

Words and Music by
ADAM SCHLESINGER
Arranged by DAN COATES

That Thing You Do! - 4 - 1

68

Verse 2:
I know all the games you play.
And I'm gonna find a way to let you know
That you'll be mine someday.
'Cause we could be happy, can't you see?
If you'd only let me be the one to hold you
And keep you here with me.
'Cause I try and try to forget you, girl,
But it's just too hard to do.
Every time you do that thing you do.

Verse 3:
(8 Bar Instrumental Solo...)
'Cause we could be happy, can't you see?
If you'd only let me be the one to hold you
And keep you here with me.
'Cause it hurts me so just to see you go
Around with someone new.
(To Coda:)

THEME FROM "THE SIMPSONS"

Music by
DANNY ELFMAN
Arranged by DAN COATES

Moderately Fast (♩ = 168)

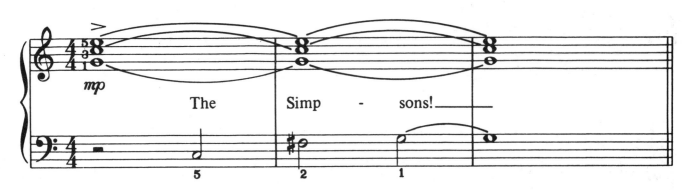

The Simp - sons!

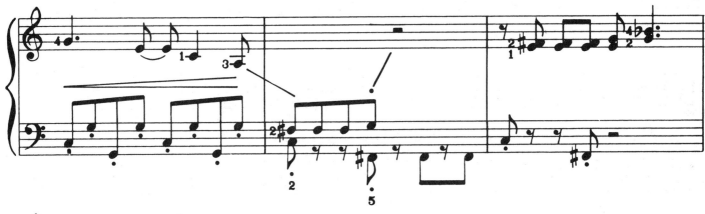

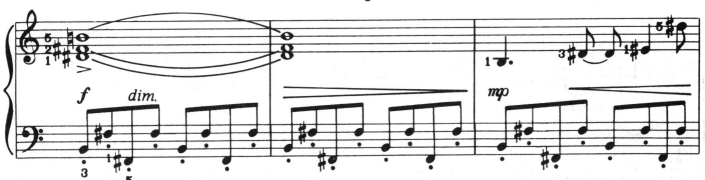

Theme from "The Simpsons" - 4 - 1

72

Theme from "The Simpsons" - 4 - 3

Theme from "The Simpsons" - 4 - 4

DUEL OF THE FATES

Music by
JOHN WILLIAMS
Arranged by DAN COATES

Maestoso, with great force

Kor - ah, _____   Mah - tah. _____   Kor - ah, _____   Rah - tah - mah.

Allegro ♩ = 152

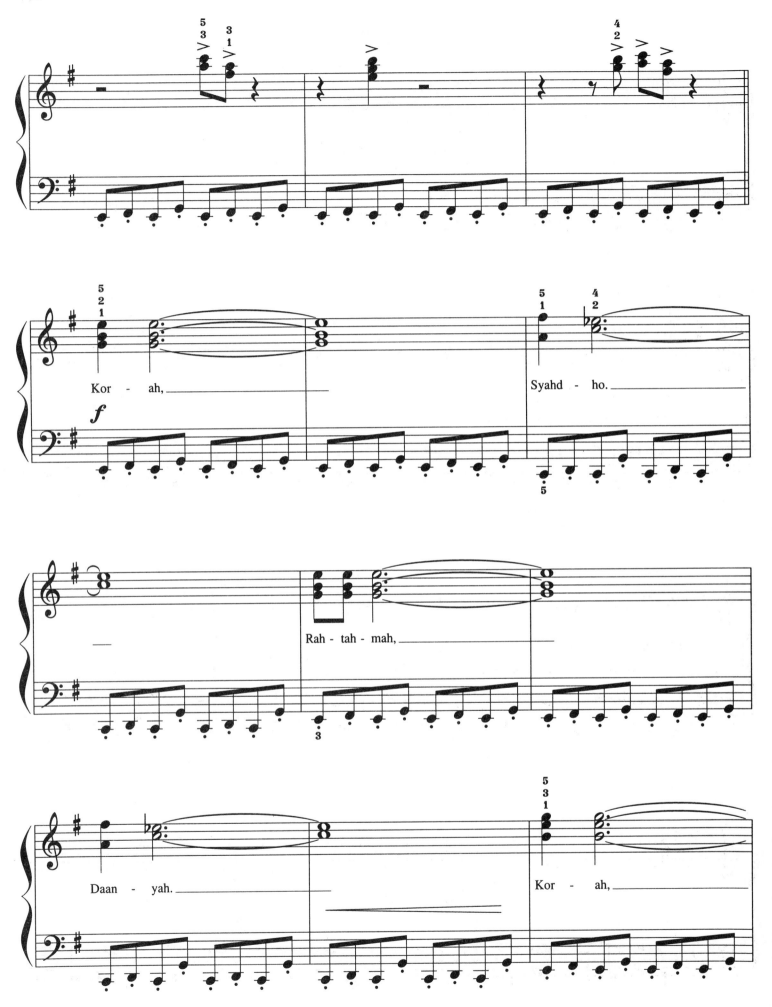

WALKIN' ON THE SUN

Words and Music by
STEVE HARWELL, GREGORY CAMP,
PAUL DeLISLE and KEVIN COLEMAN
Arranged by DAN COATES

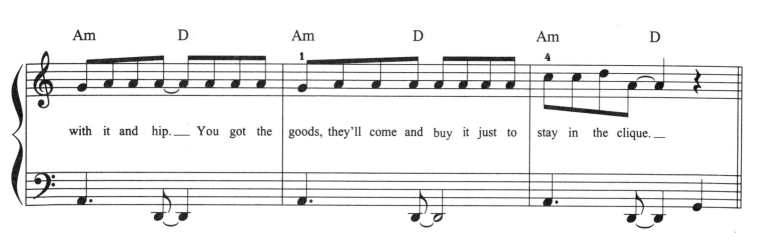

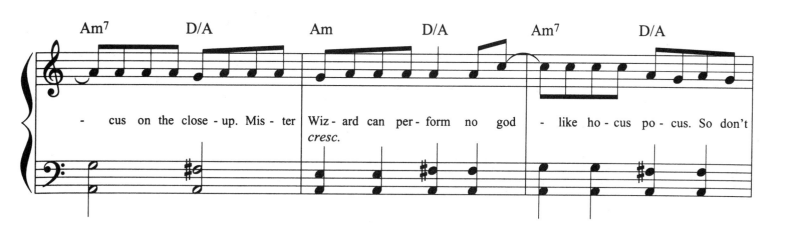

Verse 2:
Twenty-five years ago they spoke out
And they broke out of recession and oppression.
And together they toked and they folked out with guitars
Around a bonfire, just singin' and clappin', man, what the hell happened?
Yeah, some were spellbound, some were hell bound,
Some, they fell down and some got back up and fought back against the meltdown.
And their kids were hippie chicks, all hypocrites
Because their fashion is smashin' the true meaning of it.
(To Chorus:)